D1447351

In the
Absence of
Horses

PRINCETON SERIES
OF CONTEMPORARY POETS

For Other Books in the Series,

see page 104

VICKI HEARNE

In the
Absence of
Horses

PRINCETON UNIVERSITY PRESS

PRINCETON, NEW JERSEY

Publication of this book has been aided by a grant from
The Paul Mellon Fund of Princeton University Press
This book has been composed in Linotron Weiss

Clothbound editions of Princeton University Press books
are printed on acid-free paper, and binding materials
are chosen for strength and durability.
Paperbacks, although satisfactory for personal collections,
are not usually suitable for library rebinding

Printed in the United States of America by
Princeton University Press
Princeton, New Jersey

ACKNOWLEDGMENTS
"On R.L.S. and Happiness" and "The Claim of Speech" originally appeared in
Poetry and are reprinted here with grateful acknowledgment.

Library of Congress Cataloging in Publication Data
Hearne, Vicki, 1946-
In the absence of horses.
(Princeton series of contemporary poets)
I. Title. II. Series.
PS3558.E255515 1983 811'.54 83-16162
ISBN 0-691-06589-6
ISBN 0-691-01409-4 (pbk.)

for Elizabeth Saunders Hearne, M. M. A. P.

Contents

In the
Absence of
Horses

The Language of Love

So: we don't nestle weightless
In each other's hearts! The soul,
Then, is a raptor—eagle
Or falcon, and if the soul
Is a raptor some other
Soul must be prey. Is that it?

Betraying is letting loose.
The tame caged fox is betrayed
To the hounds. Or: I betray
My heart to you. Give it up,
That is, into your keeping.
Your treachery and rapture.

But we must live, too, and somehow
Understand that to love, how
To love is how to believe.
In a sacred tongue to say
"Believe" is to say "about,
At, or near to." And then, "love."

Our tongue, I mean. Fear with
Its false hieratic claims
On our flesh ignores
The tongue it speaks with as it
Hunts down the creature for whom
Flesh is always "what is torn."

Love begins as rapture. We
Began as prey, fructivores,
Tree shrews. Thus the old story
Of the harmless quivering

Beastie that discovers tools,
Weapons and at the same time

The route to Europe, will do
As well as it always has
As the story of, oh—you
Yourself. Love becomes courage
For the cannibal who must
Stay both heart and hand even

To touch the beloved with
Out leaving scars. For, always,
The touch of the cannibal
Is effective. Here's what it
Means: to have a soul, to touch
In the full heat of language.

To have a soul is to live
On the tongue, betray ourselves
By speaking up in the teeth
Of the evidence, loosing
Our hearts to the sinewy
Knowledge flexed inside our words.

Intimations of Intimacy

We would know it when it happened
By, a heroic cowboy
In good boots. He would appear
In early spring, in the pass,
His presence a sufficient
Prophesy of clear freshets
Of water cascading down,

Of the warmth of that water
And the light from its surface
In which you and I, cowboy
And mountain, would emerge at
Last as equal lights and each
Knowing all—not the forms but
The essence of each other's
Brilliance. We would welcome him,

Asking only a few dignified
Questions, as "Are the others
Enjoying the weather?" Not,
"Did anyone else survive?"
This is what we're waiting for,
Quarreling in the smelly
Pale lamplight over when to
Plant the garden and whether

He gets news in his mountain
Of our unreplenished stores.

Speech Instead of the Body

Once touched by light the skin has
It's own impetuous way
Of making plans but we were

Who we had already been
Up to that particular
Touch and then it was as though

History took us over
Or time took over from our
Bright ingenuous skins, time

With its own plans for us. You
Would rather not hear this? But
Speech is implied in moments,

Your moment and my moment,
Adroitly slipping their leads,
Passing us, and privately

Moving through each other, it
Turns out. How swiftly they will
Dance with each other, soon we

Don't see them any longer
For how they shine. I begin
To speak of it all, to speak

For my impetuous skin.

Psyche's Lamp

Because you have laid your doctrines by
In the shade of a coconut tree
Or in the honest drawer of your
Oak chest, or in your grandfather's eyes,

Because you see dolphins with your eyes
Steady, because that's what joy is,
To see with the illuminations
Of still eyes—
           The songs and the poems
Will ride your shoulders and reach to higher,
To highest, perceptions of the ant
On the leaf, the bird in his own song,
The lovers playing out evasions,
Managing to do this hand in hand.

Because you have laid your doctrines by
The spirit of vision passes in,
Out, through your lips; this is how there come
To be significances caught in
Pepper trees, clearings in the tide pools,
Leading me to arch meaningfully,
To find you out with an organized
Light, to see the god of love himself,
And to take all the consequences,
To endure all the deserts without
You, to raise my lamp again, to see
Your godhead again, to die again,
To slash the monster yet again, then
To sheathe my knife. To be a woman
Is to live with the lamp, to live with
Out the lamp. To lose you. To see you.

Here Are Lions

for Miriam Hansen

Turn now from the transparent mosses
Behind memory, behind the rocks.

Now subtle oak trees, brilliant squirrels,
Rhythmical rains, the central poem.

Now the postures of oaks, their fullness
Drawn to the earth like holiness, dream

Of the uncorruptible lion
Who takes our hearts into his jaws,

At last warm with significance.
The creature that lives beyond velvet

Greets darkness in his visions, his eyes
Announcements of the fold of the sky

In which he was born, flank, haunch, and gaze.
His paws hold out the truth of flexion.

His throat holds out long for what the mind,
Coldly on the trail of inference,

Dismisses: There are in our bodies hearts
Roaring darkly from their beds of fire.

There are in the wilderness lions,
Giants at play. For us there are ways

Of seeing, arts of ethology,
Moments of daring intimacy.

The Sanctification of Human Love

                    In heaven is
Everything foreplay
Or orgasm?
                    Well, the future answers
So many questions, not the ones
We ask, though, and a question
About the past occurs to me now. If

We had stood embracing
Beneath some burning moment
Of history, if my loins swelled
Confidently and only toward you while
Dresden, say, burned, would

That make a difference, and if it didn't
Would we keep decently still?

We did, it burned, we
Unwound our news like a waltz
Around town and the waltz added an
Undetectable brilliance to the edge
Of the flame. We come in to love

And Dresden awry, our hopeless
Ignorance of fire renewed
With every flash of insight, we play
On the outskirts feeling
Love like a garden
To walk around in and it is not
That gardens are wicked but that we must
Move closer, close enough to feel the inspiring heat,
Build walls of doubt against the flames.

Directions Taken at Night

In a while the road becomes
Two roads, at the fork. Take one
Or the other—they converge
Beyond the hill where morning
Will strike the windshield blind, so
Hurry now!
               There's a theory
About the distances stars
Take up, hanging in the pure
Sky with a crackling nearness
Touch lusts for, and the theory
Holds the inflamed wanderer
On a straight line, has come to

Hold me, fall like breath on my
Tingling skin. When I want you
I'm sightless but the theory

Takes me around the mountain
In which greedy caves pulse in
Finitely. *You must choose one*
Road or the other, says my
Kindly informant. The road

Lies singing a white oneness
Beyond the Mobil station
And you are behind me and
Before me and you converge
Again, tangled with my eyes
Beyond the hill where meaning
Pierces through the sky and spreads.

The Charge of History

Well. There you were in motion,
Angular as any buck
Charged with the creature. Desire

Was the law of your motion.
Death is the law of stillness,
Putrefaction, but we are

Changing still as we obey,
Tardily, the landscape's cry
For color and molecules

Whose motion displaces light
As swift beneath the surface
Of what we see as blood is

Beneath the surface of thought.
Thought! Transparent, pellucid,
Jaunty as a three-cornered

Sombrero beneath our feet,
Airy as love, angular
As any buck dutiful:

In your obedient skin
You are as lean as lightning,
Taut as vision on a screen,

Meaningful. Now light itself
Charges us. Definition
Comes from accepting the charge.

If Only

My vision of you: born
on bright wings

of your own crafting, but
I can't follow you

over the noise of your beauty
flapping,
                    you rise
like the man in

Judy's poem: "nakedly
beautiful." I wanted to read it,
"suddenly sexual," but now

I see. We can know
Beauty but sex like truth
Is veiled. By

Beauty? We must trust
The stunning surface while truth
crouches

eating out the center
in secret

Ana Halach Dodeach

From my mountain of words I can see
You on your mountain. Here is the plain
Between them, the text to be sponsored

By the bounding turf over which come
Tangible horses, tangible texts—
Here! For your eyes their rhythmical feet

Draw the text out in marginal airs
From your mountain to mountainous cries
Of the man who wants to live in love,

Bear fruit in his hands, in a garden
To hear the ultimate song: *Where has
Your lover gone, beautiful among*

Women? I have said he has the eyes
Of doves. *Where, o fair one, does he feed?*
He feedeth among lilies. *Where, fair*

Among women, does he feed? He feeds
At Table With Fruit, Evening With
Roses, he feeds in the valley of

The text of songs, song for Solomon,
In spicy beds over which I watch.
With my mountain of words I see Him.

With his mountain of words I am seen.

A Theory of Harmony

How we sang in the sunlit chamber!
Getting the tune wrong. The overtones
Of the small room subtly altered
The acoustics so that no desire
For the fastidiously sounded
Note could inform us. It is our song
Nonetheless, the one I will buy
A scratchy recording of some dim
Afternoon when I needn't, being
On my way to you as usual,
Humming along my way with altered
Syllables. You inhabit my throat
And are altered there as I sing you

Getting the tune wrong. Playing a clear
Sonata for flute and violin
With passion on a five-string banjo
Disturbs the violin in its case.
In later years string and bow vibrate
With a difference the musical
Score accommodates by being more
Obviously a mere guide to a
Note we are not the name of. Reading
The score will remind us, not of that
Sound dreamed by the composer, silent
In his study, but of what we sang
Instead. It is our song still, our throats,

Someone else's score. The harmonies,
As of crystal intellects, planets
Spinning like the word of God—are what
The score implies, but we have inferred
A kind of jazz, blues notes that elude

Major and minor scales, insolent
With the finesse of homeless voices.

That there is a score matters. It proves
We aren't skylarks flushed from the grass
Like bluebells in the pretty ringtime,
That we sing and know that we sing, know
That time will untune even our discords
And settle vapidly over our
Ignorant dust. This is why I fuss
Over the harmony I live with
Out hope of, why the song must go on.

What It Is About the Frog

for Colleen Lerman

That induces her
To kiss him? Well,
He has plenty

Of froggy
Appeal—that
Isn't it, though. What

Is he thinking that he
Gazes so? He has
Lived for

Who knows how long
In that pond, flawlessly
Sexual. There's a pure

Feeling in the lines
Of his posture. She feels this
And the day

Is suddenly lush. Still,
It's unusual and her gaze is not
Like his. He

Knows. She
Is taken by him. What
He knows

Is how urgent it all is
That she yield to the green
Comedy. It's all in the way he

Looks at her face so
Steadily touching her
Elsewhere.

Passing Over Your Virtues

To pass over in silence
Is to acknowledge logic,
The necessity of form,

The stunning curve of language,
The curious way it seems
To turn out that "love" means "need"

Even in a lush garden.
To pass over the Red Sea
Or your bounty—so long as

True silence and not some tense
Paralysis of the false
Is achieved—then Passover

Is always a charity,
The painted fish in the blue
Water turns to their own colors.

To pass over in silence
Is to acknowledge you if
This chatter dissolve as it

Will in the marvelous sky.

Absorbing Each Other

"I am Heathcliff"

Something taken away? Something
Transmuted? Something
To do with advice from the coach?
Is that why we shouldn't,
And if we absorb each other is it
Self absorption and
Therefore truth?

I visited the holy land
Alone, feeling of course a pain
Like amputation, knew in my side
What amputation is how it is
Final and how feelings
Trick themselves out
As history. Oh, the slow river Jordan

Had nothing to say to me nothing
Audible over the feverish murmur
Of the air nearby in which
You did not turn.

You sink into my flesh. Is
That it? Then what about
Our respective arts and duties? Oh,

We'll return to art, duty,
Even wisdom, at night as we
Turn and fall into separate breath.

The Shore

Why one goes there. What questioning from
Step to steps that form a pattern for
The quest for knowledge? Oh, this quest is

Of the middle, though it can occur
At any point of that peculiar
Peripheral vision that forces us

To stand sideways, see the path's end,
The beginning, and the empty-faced
Flowers that stand as walls. We don't see

The path itself, though. Without a clue
As to what ground supports our feet, what
Grounds have for so long upheld our feet

And hearts, we know ourselves to be in
Middle age and seek the sea for its
Independence of paths, dependence

On the marriage between its fluid
Mass and the moon's fire-fed stone. The tide's
Offspring skitter over the surface

Like wit on the surfaces of sex.
There was time before this marriage, no
Time for us, though, or any of

The other creatures born in the hollows.
Here where the joining is imperfect
The sea courts our feet, takes our terror

20

Into its heart and leaves us standing here
Intact at the edge with no knowledge
Of birthing and dying, ignorant

As our urgent skins. Why we came here:
The metamorphosis the sun has
Promised our skins, as if to sunbathe

Were to discover ourselves in new
"Exemplary states of consciousness."
The sea is married, but no example

For us. We exemplify ourselves
In our more hopeful contemplations:
Sexual knowledge is still the trope

Of completion. Your heartbeats are still
The trope of the quest. My heartbeats are
Still anxious, knowing, under alien lights

That tranform posture into a plea,
The idea that we can make sense
In our skins. The idea of sense

Marrying the unity of skin
To permanence. The sea is faithful.
We break our vows to her then return

Them, stepping at the uncertain edge,
Our postures at right angles to the
Path, catching the spray in our voices.

The Perspicuous and the Poignant

I.

Winter in California,
The sand warm, the flawless gulls

Not astonished, not even
By us. The gulls are so white

The air succumbs to their wings,
Captured by that wide balance,

That being. Benevolence
Floats in that calm way and we

Are like inept breezes soon
Stilled by the mercy of flight.

II.

Time to watch the ways of gulls:
An empathic discipline

On the wing and conclusions
Beyond theoretical

Assertions while beneath them
We would yield proudly to firm

Embracing feathers. We stroll
Quite slowly, hand in hand, through

The sand, in taut sympathy
With its delicate expanse.

III.

Suffering is implied as
A gull turns, knifes the air, slips

His beak roughly into the
Water and rises—less lovely—

A successful fisherman,
His catch weighting his jaws.

The perfections—not of gulls,
But of certain forms their flight

May take when all the air is still—
Are like a reason for hope.

IV.

The gulls prepare awkwardly
For some moment not of

The air. The benevolence
Of our postures as we pause,

No longer in sympathy
With the slog-wet expansion

Of sand, turns out to be our own.
Hope? We trudge diligently

Toward home. Thinking of gulls.
The sea is lacy with foam.

23

V.

Benevolence of posture
In time betrays everything:

The mother bends gracefully
Over her schizophrenic child,

Turns flawlessly in dim air,
And eats. The magnificent

Culture waits for her, erect,
Eager for her lips. The child

Has no posture. Without rage
We turn, try our best to weep.

VI.

We live by the seasonal
Beach, the ecological

Gulls. No singularity,
As of black holes, prevents our

Disappearing when space or
Time does. The beach is what we

Live by. The quickening of
Gulls in flight, caught in brightness

By our visions are what must
Be left to pass over us.

Coast and Walrus

Everything is larger than we can
Say, so we hardly notice the
Hazardous cliff behind us that falls

Slowly, in bits, down toward the lifeguard
At whose feet the swollen walrus bobs
In disregard of the lively child

And of us. We came for something else,
Me to live by you as though death
Had no dominion, you as though no

Fear of death had power to lounge
Behind you and lean uneasily
Against the continent. The smell stings

Like bees in the back of my skull. Here,
With nothing before the greedy eye
But rolling brine, faced with this vast, this

Uninterpretable cynosure,
We know how much we take on the faith
Of the tongue. Japan, for example,

And the restaurant beyond the cliff.
We pace the beach toward home and I can't
Speak in the thick air, so trail behind

You, embarrassed out of my creature.
Nothing speaks up from the sealed off surf.
Douleur is mute. Is pain of muteness.

II.

The tide slumps down the beach, the walrus
Trails behind us as though some question
Shimmered to be answered, a question

The sea refuses, the sea shuts her mouth,
Lets a grumble depart from her chest,
Steadily noses Walrus along,

Right behind, and a giant poem
Struggles, just there, in the ocean,
Who has closed her throat, won't speak the flash

Of the dolphins, nor all of the times
I've said that to live within an arc
That graceful would be to live in love.

How without mistake they selected
Their waves and rode them! At first we
Mistook them for sharks. Then, we saw. They leapt.

Our eyes are full. It's a beginning,
Even if they take no custody
Of Walrus. I think of taking up

Your hand and the wind is, *tout d'un coup*,
Clean and sharp. I reel under the blow
But my skin rises to it, rises

Like feathers, and I answer the sea
With scrupulous divinities, my
Syllables reach yours, your skin rises.

Modes of Speech

Sometimes I think of—about—think of
Another way of speaking with you

But with what tongue of respect and fire?
So I, or was it you, said, your eyes

Alight on it, *It remains the case, we*
Spoke becomingly, no, stuttering,

Of the pale past. Later, on a pier,
We did without the flame of language

While a quiet water widened once,
Black and orange, licked by a sunset.

Truth on the Beach

Truth wears so many guises
And is garrulous, babbles
Deep in the waters of books,

Shakes loose from our skin and flies
While the bright waves break, just
In from Japan, is a matter

Of time between here and there—
California and Japan—
Time between the two of us,

All of the others, restless,
Each on an end of time that
Packs us, each immobilized

By the guises of truth but
There is just one thing takes
The guises of light and light is

Everywhere. We swim in it,
Simultaneous pinpoints
Irrevocably uttered

At the surprised face of Truth
Who gathers her skirts and swirls
In fury, brilliant at last.

Hypocrisy and Salt Water

It's what we have to do that
Does us in the end, the pull
Of the world, nobly answered—

Or answered, in any case,
With a resolve to produce, say,
A tear, and gently refrain

From speaking. We see the sun
Through a dance of empty forms,
Through a benign atmosphere

That keeps the scorch of sun in
Its place, and dance we must or
Lose our hearts to the bare truth

Unmourning physics with her
Knowledge of the dazzle of
Cosmic entropy displays.

Study at high tide, learn a
Perfect grief as your dry eyes
Stare unmortified, dance on

A pier, or kneel by the spread
Of ancestor ocean and
Dip warm hands dutifully

Into the black and raise them

Wet to annoint your still face
With generous salt, dance so

Until you know love entire,
And dance, in time, into the
Emotional air, singing.

Morning Constitutional by
an Artificial Lake Not Located
in the Temescal Valley

I.

Leave true beauty out of it
And the lake is no longer
Alive with geese, no longer

A Lake, perhaps. Temescal
Revealed to bold (Prof.) Brewer—
This was 1861—

The loveliest maiden of
All the sultry Indians.*
Here we are, puffing along

A landscaped shore. The
Power, say the Indians,
Was long ago disrupted,

So we must learn heroic
New breathing, give the place its
Own genius once again.

* Brewer, William H. *Up and Down California in 1860-1864. The Journal
of William H. Brewer, Professor of Agriculture in the Sheffield Scientific School
from 1864 to 1903.* Francis P. Farquhar, ed. New Haven: Yale University
Press, 1930.

II.

The Indians didn't say
The part about genius,
Really, and their holy words

Languish in print as ours do
And are as susceptible
To fine interpretations,

Ever finer truths. Now we
Walk together, interpret
The shore. Which interprets us,

Of course, and there's the real rub,
The point about imagined
Bliss and interlocking hopes,

The point about faith stolen
From the industrial air.
The color schemes of breath blur.

III.

This place is not Temescal,*
But say the word anyway,
Paint it boldly on the air

* It's Lake Evans, in Fairmount Park, Riverside, California.

32

As explorers for whom some
Other lake was "alive with
Geese"* painted it on their hopes

And on a fragrant valley.
Temescal. From the Aztec,
Tema, "to bathe," and *calli*,

"Houses."† Lovely as it is,
It's not the right word in some
Important sense—I don't know

Why I bring it up even—
A bookish diversion by
A bookish lake. Take a breath.

IV.

Brewer saw the fair maiden
Not there, by the lake, but by
The hot springs, further down the

Valley. Springs, they said, that healed.
The medicinal powers
Of the springs we don't walk by

---

* Pancoast, Charles Edward, *A Quaker Forty-Niner: The Adventures of Charles Edward Pancoast on the American Frontier*. Ana Paschall Hannum, ed. Philadelphia: University of Pennsylvania Press, 1930.
† Gudde, Erwin G. *California Place Names*. Berkeley, University of California Press, 1969.

May be preserved after all
In an inappropriate
But ancient Aztec term.

Breathe it grandly on the air!
Rouse the inedible geese
Until they flap off, cackling!

Invoke what bright energies
You find here, breathe my name and
I'll breathe yours, into valleys.

V.

Valleys? Houses? How do the
Geese sleep, I wonder, when the
Park is alive with hoodlums?

Every night, all night long,
Filth, crime, terror, and dark rage
Knife the serene wilderness

Of dream. Saying "Temescal"
May not help, not in the park,
Not in my solitary

Chamber, not on the desert.
What faith we keep is kept in
Our shortened breath, embraces

Asserted as gently as
Morning asserts lake and geese
In the calm, breathable air.

34

VI.

The assertions of morning
Are as calm, clear, and bright as
Ever and insufficient

As ever they were. The lake
Ripples namelessly to our
Right, and our feet tread lightly

Beside it, leaving little
In the way of proof that we
Passed cheerfully by with our

Earnest breathing. So we must
Say something, after all, to
The air and the lake and the

Amusing geese, and say it now.
Say at least that Temescal
Was once a fragrant valley.

VII.

Say that here is a valley
Of saying where without help
Healing springs splashed in the air

Heartening our forefathers.
Say that our forefathers blessed
The ground we walk on, praying

To sufficient deities

35

Who will watch us while morning
Draws away to hard noon and noon

Gives way to harder shadows—say
That we will walk here chatting
Until we are tired enough

To rest quite safely on the
Simplified grass, panting,
Reciting translucent names.

The Ocean

Nothing applies to it but
The wind, maybe the heart—what

Else surges dangerously,
Blind to the affectionate lives

Scavenging in the hollows
Of its mind? What else? When we

Say, "That applies to the sea,
Too," we are speaking of force—

Nothing we need return to
Or acknowledge unless we

Are lovers, or artists, damp
On the edge of indifferent

Burnished waves. Then what applies
To the ocean, whatever

Brutality we may bathe
On the shore of, squealing to

Feel that sweet slap, is of us
Who dip and flirt in riptides

Applying ourselves as though
We were the clear, groundless wind.

Postcards from Jerusalem

I. First Impressions

Olive trees grow near Jerusalem,
Branching in the supple valley,
Offering penitent wood and fruit
For the crushing, oil for the light.
But I never learned Hebrew, never
Studied the small arts with which olives
Are carved out edible from the brine.
The hills seem salt-soaked, the blank rubble
To wait for something. A true weeping?

II. Missing You

Any glimmer alerted me and you
Were alert to any benign wind.
I would lean into your welcoming
Breath. The sky would gaze back and buoyant
Adonis, resurrected in blue,
Has been a brilliant pulse strolling with
No grief through my veins. Does this city
Remember your eyes? Jerusalem
Is built of bright, sensuous stone.

III. In the Beginning Was the Word

"Jerusalem, alias living
Donkeys, are plentiful . . ." *Daily News,*
1878, September
16. "Jerusalem ponies are
In high requisition." "[She] at last
Thought of trying her Jerusalem

Pony in the streets." Etc.
"Jerusalem letters: letters or
Symbols tattooed on the arms, body."

IV. Sights in the Old City: The Shops

The architecture of His eyes? The stone.
Weightless but hard olivewood carvings.
Prophets. Donkeys. Crosses. Pretty, but
No one piece suffices. I don't buy.
I never studied Hebrew but in
These streets the syllables rattle on.
The stones stand up well to the stagger
Of donkey hooves, the lion roars after
His prey, seeking his rough meat from God.

V. Sights in the Old City: The Horse

By the Western Wall a flesh-and-blood
Police horse jigs without certainty,
Thin but not truly haggard, perhaps
He gets some grain. The rider prevents
The approach of poetry as well
He ought—a timid pace prevents
Lameness. I like this horse who suffers
The city with nervous elegance.

VI. The Old City: Near the Via Dolorosa

On stone the horse seeks his elegance,
The lion and the stray cats their prey.

You can't fool a tourist, though—the gold
Is in the jewelry shops. The walls are
Made of stone, the horses of ignorance.
Olivewood toys. Some decent whiskey
Might revive my interest; I go
Hopefully seeking. God and I sit
In a cafe by the wide sepulchre.

VII. A Chosen People

I am alert to light but you are
Not here, so it is God and I who
Watch a group of Israeli soldiers
Tease an Arab vendor. Their guns swing
With their supple young movements as they
Walk away laughing, calling out,
"Suffer!" " 'Bye!" *Why do they speak English?*
Why are they so lovely? Who are they?
All God's children. I leave them to God.

VIII. A New Coming

If you were to sit here beside me
And before us were to march donkeys
Carrying New Jerusalem past
As though it were wisdom, we would merge
With God, filled with the laughter of God,
Filled with light and the inhabitants,
Accustomed though they are to holy
Rubble, would live from that moment on
With their eyes bare with astonishment.

40

IX. A Tour of the Via Dolorosa

Alone in Jerusalem I am
Led by a child whose adequate French
Is soft on the Chemin de la Croix.
The child suppresses Arabic, I
Suppress English, and our voices meet
Like clean serpents coiled among the stones.
The horse passes again, his cadence
Foreign and bright, light without art like
Our syllables uselessly nimble.

X. The City's Endurance

No vow of ours can exclude journeys
Or eternal urban visions that
Emerge from historical leavings.
With what vow could we surround the Old
City's structure? Toy crosses? A dance?
If we danced all day long, all the way
From Jaffa Gate to Damascus Gate,
We would limp home. Without you I
Lean into the liquor of God's breath.

XI. A Note on Prophesy

But I collect no information,
Really, in this unrelieved brilliance,
Even though I walk with a people
Whose prayers have the form of factual
Utterance and whose prophets still dream

In a journalism beyond time:
Here, simply, is the certainty of light
And a thousand and one tales
Told of the fathers and their dancing.

XII. Trip to Bethlehem

All of dark humanity seems a
Heavy stagger in the blanket of
God's winey breath and horses, dancing,
Beasts of half-articulate rhythms.
I can't tell God from the domestic
Shocks of life on the stones. Foreigners
Should save their dancing for home and God
Will follow. The circle we draw around the
Sacred star creates the profane life.

XIII. The New City: The Cave of the Destruction

The *idea* of such a monument,
With no song guaranteed to call us
Out again. Its sole inhabitant
Crouches in the shadows cast by soap
And candles, taunting us with the filth,
Mocking me with my fool bliss. I see
Just in time how the filth excludes you,
Even though you have a body, eyes
That wince away from cave and clutter.

XIV. The Wailing Wall

The light of Jerusalem is found
Out in Raphael; it is as though
The stones traded light the way our skins
Trade infrared, and while the soldiers
Pace before the wall, over the stones
They love, my skin moves with a soft jolt
Again. The light on the stones is not
About you. Now, to remember this
Wall of gold is to remember you.

XV. Leaving for Lod

Imagined grief and ecstasy's what
Built these magnificent walls and streets
Of stone. The real thing has worn them smooth.
He was His own architect but we
Submit to the vision of a bore
With an eye for the actual. So,
Farewell to gold, olivewood visions,
The dancing of divinities. Time
To leave this prophesy-stricken town.

The Claim of Speech

for Stanley Cavell

I.

Must we mean what we say? Stick to it,
Be bound to, chained up beside the house,

Teased by boys on bicycles, fireflies,
The seasons as they pass out of reach?

We could try meaning nothing, a way
Favored in the brightest corridors

By those who pass from life to death through
Halls of learning and replace marriage

With justice. To mean nothing is to
Have nothing at heart, to be chained up

To the right of and a bit behind
The body: without marriage, justice

Prevails as the clenched hand of culture
On the most brutal bridle prevails

Against the motion beneath that wants
To claim the hand of culture. Against

The Horse in the horse, the Rider in
The rider, the heart beneath the tongue.

II.

In the anarchies of the sensuous
Hands the order of love is leaping.

In a far corner of the landscape
A lover's hands leap in the skin's light,

And heroes' hands lap like tongues on necks
Curved with significance. The horses

Stamp and whinny, hint of caprioles
As urgently as our mute souls

And it is impossible to mean
Anything but motion. A dispatch

From the graceful landscape will arrive:
"He must be told." Lovers will obey

Thus leaving terror and time alone
To fend for themselves. I will obey,

Am obeying now, making poems
From chains, leaving the season alone—

You must be told (already your horse
Leaps beneath you!) *what you meant to say.*

On R. L. S. and Happiness

also for Stanley Cavell

I.

The fate of women is still to dream
That he returns. Dreams of the husband
Are better than dreams of the rapist

In that there is a moment of joy
Before the breakup, when the mind moves
Truculently off from the body

To make coffee. It is impossible
In either case to dream of murder,
Impossible to dream of nothing

But the moment of the dream itself
Whatever happens in the daytime.
I have a flag and lead my armies

To knowledge. I admire the flowers
Smeared golden over all my meadows.
I study Apollo. Still you toss

In your dream of Phaeton rising
Again, while in my dreams you are you,
Merely. I have no other report.

II.

Although, "My heart rouses/thinking to
Bring you news/of something that concerns
You/and concerns many men. Look at. . . ."

III.

I know the motions of the horses—
The motions of faith—and it is time
That I insist, even though the Jew

Couldn't prove he was human. Neither
Can you. I can't prove the horse, but here
Is your pain anyway, and here are

Instructions against it. It's a salt.
Consider the ocean. Consider
The infinite fishes, how they swim.

Consider us at the shore, weeping
To show our sympathy with water.
It's not enough. Only in the most

Careful details of the most extreme
Philosophies, the most careful stones
Of the breathless cathedrals, the claims

Of the most elaborate musics
On our souls do we start to dissolve
As though we had a home, and lived there.

A Principle of Horsemanship

"[For] Ben Jonson," wrote someone, "art was,
Refreshingly, hard work." I, on the other hand,
Can't speak, can't
Speak, am as hoarse
As the holocaust and move mutely
Into exhaustion, the core of my tongue
Split and vibrating.
                    When the halves are joined
Something dreadful happens. The truth
Has destroyed the world, blown up the facts
Around which space hung, the space

Through which my hand moves to take yours
In place of a creed. Now faithless, my hand
Moves eternally toward yours, battered
In the spectacular, mushrooming air.
                              Exhausted,
Glancing wildly from one half to—not to the other
    half—
(To the air between) to my hand
Turning in perfect balance between the halves
I begin—not to speak, that's all behind us now—
But to gesture. Your hand
Enters the space, or was
Always there, its secret momentum
Keeping it safe from the factual.
This is our Song and Dance—pass it,
I beg you, in silence, let the gesture
Come and go in the quiet tendrils
Of the honeysuckle vines whose scent
Stays falsely with me, or the Word
Will close in on us and move out again,
Exploding. The dance is subtle and
None but the beast may know it.

Our Condition at Twilight

At twilight our abandoned symbols
Rustle where we dropped them earlier.

Leaves that gleamed as though brilliant with our
Views of them and all our intentions—

Our plans, made in the morning, to learn
The symbolism of tulip trees—

Rattle with only our first inspired
Guesses for meaning. The wind itself

Comes to spread the mess and thus to retard
The clean rhetoric of the leaves, blur

The intent focus of the sun that flashed
On the leaves as though the sun were the

Idea. The contrasting night with
No vision in it dampens even

The whispers of what we might have known
Until we can't tell if failure is

Of us, or merely the failure of
The light. The light! That clarified

All it touched? Or chose, somehow, to touch
Only that which was already blessed

With its own insignificant clear
Edges? The leaves, for instance, edged with

Catching and radiating filaments
That held light like meaning on the lawn

And tossed it ably through the window
Onto the dim couch where we will

Rest, our forms still round, and damper than
Leaves. For now, before the dew thickens,

Our condition is this: We can hear
The leaves, blown into corners, just out

Of sight, and can just make out our forms.
I can recall that your shirt was blue

All morning and afternoon, and that
During the same period the fine

Botticelli print seemed, by means of
Its colors to be a means of truth.

The secret fluids that keep us round
In our forms will dominate the dark

As though they shone in their passageways
Luminous behind our closed eyelids.

Our condition at twilight is the
Condition of meaning as itself

A condition. The memory light
Leaves us, the knowledge that once there

Was light is the condition we find
Ourselves in when the knowledge that once

There was darkness begins to fade out.
Here we are: intimate in the dark

Where only the willful idea
We were born from, and born to, will stay

Us in our journey through the velvet
Stillness in which we will understand

That the truth is before the light and
After the light and ever more will be.

In the Absence of Horses

I. All For Love

Action is love. Once stillness
Is lost, once the surface blurs
And the lake heaves with a stone
In its heart, action failing
Is love choking and stillness

Becomes a putrefaction.
Small pulses of the murky
Water, meaningless algae,
Have force to blind the fishes
Until they leap through the air
Complete acts of silver said
In silver.
                    Action is speech
(Not speech action) the utter
Parole, its benevolence
A fusion. When focus and
Motion swiften to a brief
Rendevous, action is love
And love's the only action.

The rest is the departure
Of stillness, the glass ruined,
The lake incoherently
Shuddering

Throat and mouth shuddering can
Acknowledge nothing, something
Else comes out. To acknowledge
This is to recite, sometimes
To speak as though there were that
Obedience in our words.

II. Recital

> Because right and wrong
> Appeared, the Way was injured;
> Because the Way was injured,

> Love became complete.
> There is
> Such a thing as completion
> And injury,
> such a thing
> also
> as no completion
> And no injury. We may
> Love, or speak, or until
> Death abstain from completion.

Something has been said. With our
Words we form recitals. In
Our recitals we stand forth,
Heirs apparent to the world.

III. Argument with Samuel Daniel

". . . not the contexture of words
But the effects of action
That gives glory to the times"

But the contexture of words
Is action

IV. *Courage,* Cry the Inmates

Now hurt speaks its circular
Language. Spasmodic, obsessed
With origins the tongue of
Damage thrusts acrobatic

Syllables up its own ass,
Holed up in the certainty
Of imprisonment. I mean

Ordinary damages:
"My finger hurts," or, "He left
Again," or, "My father is
Still trying to murder me."
Such damage is hard to speak
Of, but speaks anyway, so
Plain are our appeasements and
Black.
        But we make our decisions

About who speaks and in what
Fading or expanding light
The speakers stand. We can say,
Let us go to the park and
Stand upon the ground awhile
Until we come up at last
With something totally new and
True to say.
        Damage speaks
In circles, but the human,

Speaking of and from all his
Hot hurts, can speak up, move up

And out, finally, not out
Of damage, but out of the
Darkness of thought, its bondage
To the facts.

Merely naming the facts leaves
Them behind: Speech gestures at
What we were and rises thus
To a universe beyond
Speech. Once beyond speech we find

There is an action of speech
At the center of all our
Acknowledgments and we are
Ourselves after all, damaged,
Brutal, and speaking, brutal
And pure.

V. More on the Question of Anguish

On whether in the poem's
Flesh a grain of sand, fester
Of foreign object, foreign

Pain. Whether to heal, embrace,
Press softly, is to suck out
Bitter brightness of language,

Relieving that pressure. Whether
The Beloved's dewy breath
Eases completely the song's

Heart, refreshes the desert
Until we live without words
In an evening of roses—

Or there is less, beginning
As a query about the rose,
Single and distant, clearly

Nothing but a rose and truth
The desire for roses when
The desert is black with light.

Whether or not one action is
A rose or the glitter eyes
Take on in the desperate

Parchment of these violent
Sands that shift, grumbling, and toss
Miracles of intention

Up before our eyes. But such
Questions may not be answered:
Here, in the grass, are horses.

VI. Digression

A fish, ascending, affirms
Gravity: Head and tail point,
Plunging, to the earth, actions

Are made by their syntax, the
World is made available
In the syntax of a fish.

The fish, like a syllable or
A real poet, inherits
The earth and in one motion
Gives it away.
                    Desperate
Movement is not an action:

A horse stumbles along. Edge
Of a leaf rots in the grey
Wind. A man, telling a lie,
Breathes on the mirror, disturbs
The surface.
                    In the fogged glass
A child or an artist will
Trace the liar's name, tracing
Pardon for horse, leaf, life.

VII. Beyond Fishes: Mare and Foal

Here, in the grass, are horses.

When the foal lay curved, brooding
In the dark mare, his feet fringed,
Softened, action was stillness,
Stillness the only action,

Until she broke sweatily
In the ignorance that cries
Out of itself. Now their heads turn,
Each toward each other, the mare's
Head and heart dance, the foal's head
Dances this way and that way—
Becoming actions in that
Symmetry. What becomes them

Is that each horse is dancing
Within and surrounded by
The other's eyes: Now their hooves!
Blaze into definition.
They surround the light, outlined
Against the clear wind, knowing
What they mean. See how the heart,
Defined in its lake of blood,
Turns this way and that, rising
To show ever new facets
Of damage. Consider the mind,
Turning in the congealed air
To catch each dancing facet
Until it can contemplate

The whole heart in its motion
And make it whole. The pale foal

Stumbles in the wind, numb in
The wind until he dances
Between the mare's gaze and ours
For wholeness. He eats boldly,
Bruising the grass, and the grass
Shines in the wake of his teeth.

VIII. "That,"

Fish and lake shine in the wake
Of the dance, teaching us that
The past is gone, is become
The past; terms for the snows
Of l'antan; meaning's the first
And last valor of language.

Our delicate studies of
The hidden parameters,
Spaces in equations for
Unpronounceable details
That slosh along without us,
Yield the information that
The present of love is an
Act, an utterance swift and
Prompt. The present sky holds back

Blue in a saucer. The lake
Reflects without knowing
Refractory spectrums. So,

IX. In the Absence of Horses

Our study is poetry,
Is the art of the horseman
In whose gaze the world dances,
The art of the mind finding
The heart turning in the press
Of the mind. The horse enters
The turn of the heart. The heart
Enters the turn of the poem.

Higher thoughts than these exist
And higher questions edged with
Silver, but find no higher
Answers lest you turn your clear
Horseman's gaze from the dancing
World and leave the foal crumpled
In a hot shadow. The act

That broke the surface beneath which
The unpronounceable still
Sloshes breaks open ever
More brilliant surfaces. To
Say the eyes may lay their claim
To any more than this, to
Some orange interior, some
Heart of Africa, some
Flaming core of dark truth, is
To dissect the optic nerve,
Leave the mind to move blindly
From inference to brutal
Inference. The brow's clear lines
Inferred from the nether shapes
Are not instructions, reason

As you will of horses, so
Careless on their hoofy legs.

In the absence of horses
The Beloved will suffice
And will change on the brutal
Turns of the tongue, becoming
The Betrayer, betrayed, and
Hollow figure of fullness
For seventeen years until
At last lovers, abandoned

Again to their gazing are
Figures of knowledge, figures
Of action for which any
Steady emblem is enough
And any time, time enough

For the world opens gently
With the song in its embrace.

Night Track

We had ideas, the dogs had ideas, and the world
shouldered abruptly away like a rabbi
on Christmas Eve. We were
lonely hunters praying to the caverns
of hounds, knowledge in their flews, the night
swift and black.
                    Lonely hunters?

the summer settled and
rose again delicately
lapping at my breasts

but there was a wind problem, the dogs
leaping into the wind, we followed: god
in a field of god leaping into god's breath found

a lost child, a rabbit, a criminal, empty burrows

(god)

the dogs closing the gap and no
fictions in that field, that
summer we were to have been in love
but closed the gap instead and lived
in the crystal wind, not
for the quarry

found god anyway

turned from your breath, turned from my breath,
gulped the fleshless air,
turned from your loins, from that story

66

no womb-fruit, no fictions, god

in a field of god, no study
of our seasonal graces, recited the wind
not in our sleep
                    we turned in pure
focus, unblanketed in the shifting stars, steady
at the center of the dark wind

II.

The thing we liked about tracking
was not daring to make mistakes: *hound's
gotta hold that line, run that fox
all the still night*, no noise, no lullabies

no stopping for logic
                            just one music and *the logic
of the inheritance that put that bugle
in the hound bitch's throat*, angels
and the scents oracular

at the end of the run quiet
hands, silken ears, our flesh
become a brilliant nocturnal creature
in which we would live forever

and still do. Morning
slumps at our ankles. We live on,
Restless at the end of the run.

False Spring

I mean any Spring, any
Strawberry, any cloud glazed
Like a ham with sugary
Unnatural heat, any
Throat choked with the poetry
Of love, desperate in its
Refutation of mankind's madness
And kindness, refutable
As all denial. I mean
All I have written, promised,
Seen and lived with that narrowed
Gaze I mistook for vision.

Vision alert, full of the
Prompt and generous morning,
The suchness of hoofy colts,
May be Spring. Vision counting
Itself Spring is not Vision
And not Spring. Vision counting
Itself at all is the heart
Hurrying by the present
Encounter, gluttonous for
Its own past. But see what hovers
At the peripheries of our
Shoes: Symmetries of, say, seals

Who with unplanned angles of
Light stun us, declare their forms
Without choreography.

Entropy: *Wandeners Nachtlied*
for Ada Schmidt

Überhaupt intersection of tongue
And soul. Of course, and above all that,
And above all the mountaintops,

That lively calm, full of green panache,
The small birds know. *Ruhest du auch*, but
Meanwhile love is finished by mistake

While we are considering the way
We might ask about our pain and to Whom
We might clearly direct such questions.

Above the mountaintops there is calm.
The little birds are hushed in the woods.
In the treetops breath can scarcely be

Feared. *Ruhest du auch*, but the treetops
Flame and tumble in the storm; action
Before philosophy is one right

Answer to such falls. Love is complete
By accident or else by mistake, love
Has in either case no justice

To it, and there is in our august
Syllables of justice far too much
Unacknowledged love. When I say this

I do not mean that heart and reason
Are not what we live on—how we live
By thoughtful love has been covered in

Other texts. Just now I want to say

That our living and our dying, too,
Are both in defiance of the laws

That spin the cosmos, that as outlaws
We must probe each other and thus prove
Our thieve's honor and our urgent love.

Toward a Cultural History

We made the ones who trot, backs
Flawless and bare to the wind.
In that wind evenness of stride
Was a theological
Elegance. We drew the loins
Long on the high descendants
Of Sham and ploughed supple turfs
Before their hooves that they might
Reach infinitely to a
Significance of thundering.
We prayed for the gathering
Of hooves into corners tighter
Than the panic of cattle

And still the horses dodged us
Like fireflies. We prayed to their
Refined bones, built palaces
For horses, horses around
Palaces of certainty,
Nations around palaces,
Gardens around bleak pastures

And forbade the bitter wire
For the fences, and weeping.

Now the grooms and the women
Kneel at the ragged center
To study pathology,
Alone with the actual.
The names of the bones betray
The grounds, the architecture,
The king whose insomnia
Is a state secret. Within

Their hooves inflamed coffin bones
Swell rebelliously and burst
Through their soles, lie on the world's
Surface, glowing like our hearts.

An Historical Note: Staghounds

Early in the time of the griffon's
Actual existence, we crafted
An odd holiness. There were whelped long
Hounds, with a vision that could love the
Shy, subtle motions of light left by
Deer in those forests of softening
Horizons. Searching by deerlight, hounds
Lengthened into the branching calmness
Where nothing at all was owned except
By knowledge (as of the plans smaller
Creatures made in the civil mosses).

In a forest made lucid by deer.
As if leaves were a plan for a text
Illuminated by feral monks
Who would keep their vows even though the
Light might harden against them. In that
Wide forest text hounds stopped reading
The paranoid old wolvish custom
Of huddling in dens. How kindly they
Bounded, predators as always but

Now with what dreamy, elegant strides!

Sappho's Parchments

a translation

Songs, all seeds, scatter sweetly like oats.
Beauty flies as we tell it and leaves
Our tongues to rattle with the bone-dry stalks.

To tell of Sappho is to tell of
These parchments that wrap the dead. Within
Their eyes enlarge secretly, like songs.

The Moral for Us

Never trust servants, that's the
Shabby moral King Midas
Kept with him and earnestly
Told the curious poet
Who came with ulterior
Motives. And whispers of this?
The benevolent donkeys
Still graze, tossing furry ears.
Silver winds whistle through each
Ear, and ear of corn, and head
Of wheat and shimmering blade
Of grass. We listen, leaning
Forward over our yellowed
Copies as though they told us
Holy secrets and not the
Feeble gossip of poets—
Some noble new truth. Gossip
Will endanger no furtive
Listeners. Let us eavesdrop,
Rather, on the perilous
Dreams of royalty who in
Their sleep turn visions to gold.

The American Dream

for Jim Weaver

It happens in the daytime, requires
Magnificent vistas that argue
A careful focus near to but not

Exactly on the point where beauty
Does her famous acrobatic flip,
Flinging terror loose. And whether "frightened"

Means betrayed by picturesque cages
Built flimsily by workmen who knew
Better, or by the ordinary

Mechanics of seeing, matters less
Than the technologies we invent,
Trying for love, standing on a rock

And speaking to the rock, or praying
For entry, praying for horses that
Break it, open poems, word for word,

From which we get a view of the sea.
It is our rock, built by our full hearts.
The rock is all we have to stand on.

Listen to the song it fails to sing.

After Mandelstam

Quiet! No longer do I
Encourage the active word
Forward; the air these days
No longer flames at the touch
Of my motion and still I

Have no feel for the crooked
Lines of peace, and now your mouth
Twists, empties:
                        The signal
Of my humiliation.

Hush up! Nothing sings but time
In the sizzle of embers.

Lesson

I will show you a horse, place
You around the horse so you
Circle with Horse at center
Instead of birth, death, love,
Or the best that has been said.

You will see that while the horse
Is finite still the universe,
Shed in fragments by his hide,
Is infinite, is the gift
Of the horse of the center.

For the sake of exercise,
The fill of haunches, I'll put
You at center, send the horse
To circle, you'll be shedding
The universe while horse and

Universe discover you.

Song for the Eye

Perhaps not hope, even if

Power grows in the subject
Of the sentences about
Horses, and you, my dear, say

No, maybe not, maybe no
Hope, the horses "dance" only
In an imagination

And things imagined and things
Real are not on a par. No.
Or, isn't the nowhere man

A bit like you and me? Why
Then are the hooves of the damned
Horses drumming actual

Musics on actual grounds
For belief? And someone hums
Along, keeping time. The horse

Is the copula. The world
Interlocks our words with one
Soft click the very moment

Your hand becomes actual
Between my thighs, O, other
Connections come in for true

Turns of praise, so if your eyes

Are nothing like the sun then
The best song is of the horse

Whose delicate feet can touch
The eye without leaving scars.
The song will sound when your eyes

Open to the horses' hooves.

The Boy and the King

The soul and the sovereign presence
Square off against each other, squaring
The castle of the grail into which

You stumbled, thinking it was the side
Of the mountain or else your own side
And an ordinary wound. Your eyes

Glance left and down. To stare at them full
Would be to know terrible hungers
For lions and for the sun their king,

For the prior face of the sun, that
Audible light in which both speech
And sight greet in the active throat, the

First light, its incomprehensible
Mass from which come lions, books, and your
Eyes. Seek out that light for only it

May return your gaze. Before the split-up
Into eyes and ears there had been flames
Of being in which we had lived long

Before questions about *here* and *there*,
Earth and *sun*, even *you* and *me*,
Were invented. Attend to the sun.

Stare at its crackle and joy and hear
The roar of the light in the furnace
Of your desire. In the lion's heart

After which you falter, soul in flame,

In the beast whose darkness is brilliance,
God and your performance will be one.

Cat Canyon 2 mi →

Everything beside the road
Is so gentle. The spaces
Between the oak trees are filled
With California, so where
Are lions? The mute horses
Graze in placid poses, not
In paintings by Stubbs, but we
Who know how to read the sign
Must conclude that two miles off
Terror and beauty couple,
Cleave each unto each, become,
Through the laws of form, one flesh.

The irresistible force
Of imagination burns
Beneath the hood, wedded to steel,
Carrying us along with
Its complete explosions, and
We fear no evil. Our cat
Purrs beneath its glowing hide.

A Word Against History

You said *poet* when everyone else
Was about to say *soldier* and wait
For stalwart trees to yield a cache
Of restored songbirds, exactly winged,
Songbirds from whom the soldier receives
Versions of a taut theme of courage.
The soldier mounts and there are no wings
Anywhere, the tree churns, the poet
During both wars studied vacant leaves,

And some soldiers came in time to lean
Beneath the tree's silences on nothing
But what they could say about the horse,
That his heart beat separately while
Dragons compelled union. Victory
Tore out the soldier's heart. A torn heart
Is what I now have to give away
To the tree's reticence, reticence
Is all we give to the street's sorrows.

Wholeness would speak. A whole poet, whole
Soldier, between them, could hear the songs
And the cries in the streets and the change
In the leaves as a suddenly loud
Wind stirred them. With torn hearts
Unmoved by the wind we parody
Advances, speak from erotic shells
Syllables that have no force to touch
The flanks of our shivering soldiers.

Without the soldier who stands, shoulders
Held *thusly* in the actual air
Of the place the horse boiled and festered
In a poet's excessive mix of

Exhaltations. The soldier chooses
Whom he will fight when the choice is pressed
Like clothing, and in his husbandry,
Studied in the moving cold, chooses
With whom he will live in peace. His death

On gory grounds seems to serve the life
Of the horse only in the poet's
Mad syllables torn from dangerous
Corpses of leftover origins.
The reticence that follows madness
In its first discovery of leaves
Is what we live in and what must be
Revised in saner tropes of breathing
Matched to the horse's large sure motions.

In this extremity of branching
Stillnesses it is something, a change,
A stirring of canonical airs,
To have breathed, to have muttered *poet* when
Everyone else meant to say *soldier*,
Something to be said against lions
When we mean something else but have gulped
In the quiet that waits for soldiers
To fall, vacant under songless leaves.

Gauguin's White Horse

There he stood, quite suddenly,
Innocent nose to foreleg,
Bent against no betrayal,

As though all the gods had laps
And were not inflamed. Shadows
Bore fruit. Edible mosses

Exhaled an eternity
Of breath. Someone asks whether
Gauguin held his when this horse

Flowed out into the foreground
Like an ethics of texture.
Now, it matters. We, with our

Breath as heavy, as rapid
As paint, reach to pluck the horse,
Letting time back in, and take

Flesh for the trope of the horse,
The horse for a trope of grace,
Perception in place of the

Acts of the heart, for granted.
It was all actual. Here,
The emptied frame has become

What fills in for the prior
Question—not the one about
Wanting our innocence back,

Or how to send it forward,
A wisdom of matted manes,
Nor where the laps of the gods

Fall to when the sun rises.
The question is behind mouths
And won't come out of the frame

As long as we keep choking.
Ease in your throat is what lets
The head of the white horse swing

Downward through air, toward water.
Ours are the mouths Gauguin's brush
Bends to, compelled to answer.

Canvas with a Bit of Tyger Showing

Without myth? Without emblem?

They prowled, then, in the first trance,
Neither noble nor debased.
Theirs was the trance of attack,

The trance of eros inflamed,
And the trance of predation.
So what was dark, original,

Prior to the need for truth,
Was bred in the tyger trance
Of analysis. Bred there

In a heart fully exposed
To a light it owned alone.
They happened before crime did,

Their forms occurring under leaves
That guarded them from wisdom.
There was one intent upon

A shaft of sun. The only
Right thing for you and me to
Say, was: Stay out of the light!

It had to be said softly
Or the attention of the
Brigher tygers would enclose

Us immediately. This
Was no performance, no sign
Linking boundaries, no tie

Between souls. We were either
In their light and therefore not
In our own, or we stayed back

On the fruitful plain among
The placid enquiries of
Courteous hooves, devising

Speculations on the leaves
Through which the light of tygers
Filtered. It was not for us.

Or, if it was, that meant no
More of the plain, the hooves, the text
We made of leaves. No more cat

In the corner before which
Pranced the horses in *haute école*.
Art had to do with keeping

Cats off, with building the halls
In which real horses danced their
True revelations of form.

We put the matter aside,
Focussed on the drum of love.
It takes awe before hooves,

A feel for the domestic
Pussy and a new terror
Of the facts before we learn

To paint hoof and paw without

Leaving one or the other
To savage intimacies.

Nigger and Dragon

for Harry Lawton

Nigger had a heart, and there,
Curled in an unspeakable
Elegance, slept dragon who

Dreamed of the contingencies
Of flight, stirring up his wings,
Nervy with iridescence

And as he stirred up he stung
Nigger. The stars leaned in on
Dragon's sleep for the dear sake

Of contingent gleaming, for
Their hunger for nigger's heart
Blood that, buried in its flow,

Glowed back at dragon, oh glowed
Heartless and there were monsters
Blanketing nigger's noontime,

Nightime, choretime; blanketing
The world in its uneasy shift
Before God. When nigger cracks

The world is suddenly bare
Before dragon, bare before
Her lord, the lord at her heart,

The merciless lord of whole
Niggers, lord at the center:
Now, with mercy gone, the world

Dances before God as though God

Were love. Nigger, cracked open,
Finds a beloved—or, the

Beloved finds out nigger;
The god of love suffuses
Their breath with what was always

Known and feared, how a dragon
Lives in and on our flesh with
No flame of need. The beyond

Of the dance is God who stands
Quite still, without breath. Who stands,
Seen by iridescent eyes.

A Mirror for Magistrates
for Jo Miles

I can hear the dogs bark as I write and since
They are outside, perhaps you can hear them too.

You try to call, but, "The number you have reached
Is haunted." And after that, how can the line
Go on? But it does, as you see, continue.
From it ensue dolphins, ghosts, shabby monsters,
Here and there visions, as of your perfect way
Of moving toward me, and somewhere above all
Love darting in and out among the enjambments
That carry us past love, back into shadows.
Love, mounted on horses that see in the dark
Makes its own way through the poem as we make
Ours. I walk along, griefless, grieving for grief—
Or is that you I see about to compose
The world around a single swift stanza: *A*
Man and a woman and a blackbird/Are one.

"The American Oriole is merely
A blackbird." A man, a woman, a blackbird
And the American Oriole are one
And therefore true, true and therefore one—being?

One thought, the thought we sing when we live ourselves
Toward the blackbird. Let's put it another way:

A rider and a horse are one. A rider
And a horse and a magistrate are still one
For there is only one vision to see them,
One name to name them, one song to move them from
Left to right across the perfect Italian
Landscape It is their motion in the landscape
That makes them real, or one might say their motion
In the mirror makes the landscape real, the ground

Substantial beneath their single—singular—
Praise of the Italian airs and the graces
By means of which they live on, becoming one.

A man and a haunted telephone are one.

A horse, a man, a woman, and a haunted

Because Your Cat Is Dying, Naming Is Not Yet Complete

for Diana Garber

Poems written to be found in rooms
The poet has vacated or else
Never understood. That's the modern

Of it, the jagged line, composure
Without heroes in a world that still
Needs them. Also their jaunty horses,

Also their wrathful grooms, the justice
That singles out truth and disappears
In what it finds. All the implosions

Required in Venice, the noble Moor
To rise again and choke up again—
The poets need heroes for the text

From which nothing can be selected,
And lovers need the text of the sun
In order to mouth their origins.

With or without the text war goes on.
With the text the war is remembered
Quietly, without the righteousness

Of reconstruction, the irony
Of historical fact. The fiction
Of the world without God must go on

Until your gaze collapses before

The clarity of the stars, the wind
Of the Beloved as he dances

Without stars in just the solitude
Of truth. All of this must happen
In the morning, the true dawn that comes

Darkly, escapes the myth of sunrise,
The texts of love. Now the body turns
Inward to the center of the dream

Of nothing. Love encloses the air
Until speaking with its new motions,
Its significance of galaxies

Wakens us and God is born again.

A View of Motion

Your eyes, ruined by calamaties,
Jerk in the corners of bare chasms;
You announce a rotted frailty
And look away, will not stay to look.
Madness jets through the air, the red flies
Buzz insignificant hot torments.

Steady eyes confiding what they see
To what they see were the one power
Love had, shattered by a single jerk
With which both center and cynosure
Were wrenched apart as the sky, flaming
With flies, leached the earth with mockeries.
My dull throat spasms, it is I who
Cannot say that all the while there are

Passage and *volte* and *serpentine*,
The horse made more visible with strides
That are sure of the earth and beat out
Unfluttering acknowledgments, life
Announced out loud to the giddy leaves.
This poem of the only instinct
That dance steadily now transumes
Desire in ceaselessness and power
Made light as air by balance. Massive
Shoulders made buoyant in any light,
Any soft inquiry that attends
To the generosity of a form
That intervenes between the crumpled
Earth and the ruined eye, shaking off
Shape after shape until earth and eye
Are full and the erratic red buzz
Of flies is a peaceful glimmering
That sings, "Sense, sense," of, beyond, and before

The weightless blue and the weighted black
Of the sky. It is as though the stars
Were present in a foreground of light
To take up the project of the heart.

The hooves recite unending candors
And mean a possible beholding,
The restored eye of the heart restored
To the eye, a movingness that can
Move the eye, all that I cannot say
Against your rapture of unsuccess,
All, perhaps, that I will come to say.

The Search for a Word with Only One Meaning

for Robert Tragesser

Not a unified field theory of the throat and the resonances that attack it like prayers against God's momentarily fitful sleep.

Not something as linear as pedagogical hope, or the answer to the question that replaces guilt, at last, with the facts of what we all said.

Not something that, like the responses in a cathedral, has meaning only in a texture of certain architectures and postures.

Even the word that placates the statesman and moves him into a greeting as true as yours and mine will not do.

Even a word learned on a mountain, a word that makes the naming of oneself into an action, even that won't do, for it is only the cue for a shift in point of view.

Horses, or dancers, or lovers, speaking up as though to reveal that they speak were to live in a wind restored to the music of the spheres—this gives an idea of what I mean, of the word proven in its motion in the world. But this is not what I mean.

"Goodbye," though it allows us to turn both toward and away from our destinies and each other, all at once, as though the straight line of fate were an optical illusion, turns out to be more than one word, and "God be with you" assents to division in the stars.

And I may mean the first Word, but that is beyond the poem now. The poem can only remember it helplessly, can only profess so much faith. The theatre is empty and so echoes too accurately, without transuming, what is uttered there.

The poem wants, though. The poem wants. A word so archaic we could not help but utter it. Then helplessness would be enough.

Ierushalayim Shel Zahav*

for Colleen Lerman

All of my lovers dance in your hands
getting it right at last as your skin
seeks me out and is brighter
in my chambers than the creatures
with sharp feet and soft eyes

and once in a while we are lucky
find a hill that is steep enough

our feet become real in the ascent
the path is wide enough for both of us

because we are not goats we sometimes
need to know that we are not goats
our only nimbleness that of waiting,
endurance, you said, and perhaps it's true, but

In Jerusalem I met a man who gave silver
away to thieves. Later, in California, a poet
read her poem of the feet of dinosaurs
uttered in the golden hills, informing us
and today my daughter moves quietly into prophecy,
a flame in the house, says, "That was our friend Motke
who gave silver to thieves, who found
the footprints." They said he could give silver
to thieves, and he did, and Jerusalem
glitters on her hills in that light, and Motke
dances there, I think, for how else

---

* "Ierushalayim Shel Zahav" means "Jerusalem Of Gold." It is the title
of a popular Israeli song, very lyrical and tender, which the Israeli
soldiers sang in 1967 when they took over the Old City.

could he *see*? and somewhere there are thiry Jews*
with sharp feet and soft eyes. The trouble
with the hill is not that it is empty of deer
but that it overflows with meaning
wherever we put our feet. The hill—I mean,
Jerusalem, what lies outside the world
and is the value of the world. There is no escape
from the gleaming hills of the city.
Its inhabitants cannot sin it away. Some of them
see this, and today my daughter glances
at the poems of the American poet. They are not
for her, but even as she lays the book down
in the wrong place the city inspires her breath
with the gold that gushes from the hill
when the creature bruises its surface. Look, I mean
that the children of the Arabs are torn,
torn, are less than the food of wolves, that
every pilot is an archangel; we cannot
turn from them while their relentless planes
surround the sun, and, true form to their forms
murder comes after the lines in the poem
where all of my lovers dance in your hands
getting it right at last, that you
and you, and you, whoever you are
still seek me out and will remain brighter,
brighter. And somewhere there are those thirty
Jews, and the song will end on a hill
where nothing will dim its nimbleness

* Refers to a sometime tradition that there are thirty good men in the
world, and that the world will cease to exist if any of them should
cease to be good.

PRINCETON SERIES OF CONTEMPORARY POETS

Other Books in the Series